THE KNOPF POETRY SERIES

Man in the Open Air

Man in the Open Air

POEMS BY

Stephen Sandy

ALFRED A. KNOPF NEW YORK 1988

THIS IS A BORZOI BOOK
PUBLISHED BY ALFRED A. KNOPF, INC.

Owing to limitations of space, acknowledgments for permission
to reprint previously published material appear on page 85.

Special thanks to the Ingram Merrill Foundation; to
The MacDowell Colony, Blue Mountain Center, and
Alfred University, for their assistance; and to
Karen Latuchie, for hers.

Library of Congress Cataloging-in-Publication Data

Sandy, Stephen.
Man in the open air.

(The Knopf poetry series ; 28)
I. Title.   II. Series.
PS3569.A52M36   1988   811'.54   87-45230
ISBN 0-394-56312-3
ISBN 0-394-75572-3 (pbk.)

Manufactured in the United States of America

FIRST EDITION

IN MEMORY

E. M. S.

A. F. S.

Contents

I

Letter from Stony Creek

Ground zero all at once; after rain, this brightness.
The hollow sea grass hummocks thump when I
Jump down, or kneel to gather glasswort, red
And cold. Blue juniper, rose hip, towering reed
Plume in eyes, ears, nose, here at the quarry,
Crater of water mantled with green and one duck;
Granite cubes long gone to the Statue of Liberty.
Behind, the Sound gleams on Mr. Kingsley's cottage,
Light off the water ablaze on the twill of slates.
Slimmed by the sun behind her, a woman is riding
Her bicycle on the pier. See, she is on the waves!
I want you to picture the cars in line to the city,
To Monday; now, the obvious ease of all, if only
For a moment. Experience itself is a cul de sac.
Depths in the rock beckon. Lichens peel, and you
See in. The light on the water trembles; rises.

Ray's Garden Shop

Bony Ray Plummet
at the end of Center Road
    on the Hoosac shore

among the willows
around his lean-to raised plants
    and vegetables

junipers, vinca
(and other ground covers) a
    "specialty," which he

sold from his dooryard
to local farmers and such
    as found the dirt road.

A modest living,
Ray in his *Hood's Milk* warm-up
    jacket would say; you

won't believe it, friend,
I'm in retirement here.
    In pink on blue boards

he was daubing signs
about his sturdy myrtle,
    his delphinium,

squatting in the dust
which spread over his lean arms,
    his seedlings and his

long array of signs
announcing the quality
    of his flowers, more

bountiful words and
more colors than his flowers.
    He stood to shake hands

warming to the chance
visitor, making ready
    to chat his ear off.

Winters this place gets
too cold, so I take off; drive
    down to Florida:

he pointed to his
sedan, half garaged and half
    disguised with creeper.

How odd it was, but
we must pass the time of day
    if I did not buy

or if I did. He
was too cheerful and too weird
　　for me. I was hot

to get out of there,
when his hand gripped my elbow.
　　He dropped to his knees

and said, I don't know
what your beliefs are, I don't
　　want to offend you

but I believe that
heaven and hell are right here
　　on this earth. Mind you

I'm no *atheist*
but, see, after flesh-and-blood
　　it's bye-bye, baby.

Incidentally,
friend, just look, this marvelous
　　stuff growing away

right on the shoulder
right in oil and sand and all
　　this dust. He bent his

old dry body down
and held a head of dust-white
    hens-and-chickens for

me to see. This here
is it, he said. I gave him
    a hand and he stood.

You're kidding me now,
I said. We grinned and hugged while
    a car, as surely

as the dawning of
manly knowledge in a boy,
    came on, down the slow

road, a leading edge
trailing a fresh plume of dust
    toward Plummet's garden,

like the shadow of
a cloud moving overhead
    across the sun and

drawing a dark squall
over the bowed grass, the white
    and shivering leaves.

Egyptian Onions

Athwart, nudging each other,
The fat Egyptian onions teeter
As if they were dozing on guard
In the garden of Ceres; stiffen
And pale, contending with aster
And ragweed, each plump column
Flaring, bowed with the weight
Of its berry-bunch capital; a little temple
Sprouting the ruin of itself.

Blisters of tiny onions, bitter
Lilies, nod to the wind,
White wisps of minuscule root hairs
Curling in the afternoon air
Like the thinnest beard of the wisest sage,
Like the vestige of yearning for darkness,
Loose skeins trolling the air
That yet might fall
To the fuming soil; and drink; and begin.

O, Mrs. Gale

for Ben Belitt

"Essential toilet articles bring"
She wrote, and going through his things
"He calls his hero Isosceles"

Murmured. O, he knew how to please
Till he made Caliper Valley sing
His praises; his little universe,

His coltish legs as he ran in a game!
It is Caliper, it is Denniston,
It is Mrs. Gale there breakfasting,

It is the morning on which young Gale
Will be taking a turn for the worse.
"Devotion to animals, flowers, praise

For the permanence of favorite places,"
She writes when he begins to fail,
". . . his hobbies, his tall hankerings."

That night she dreamt of her own bath,
Clawfooted tub half warm, half full;
She dreamt she was an ancient dame

Two thousand dreamy years ago
In Egypt, enjoying unnumbered days
As the desert cut its pre-emptive swath

That left stone walls illegible
And milled the deep-carved marble faces
To lumps. When she wrote, "those years ago—"

It seemed perfectly clear. Not so
"This last month—" scrawled below. The one
Was a brick, the other a vapor. And more,

One was the truth, like her hat left where
She dropped it on the hospital floor
Under a folding metal chair.

Command Performance

for Robert Lowell

There was no mound to mark your burial
When the Russian poet wandered there,
Backing away to gaze at the flame sky.

The tears you blinked back filled your eyes
The day we came to cheer you up.
You lay across that bed like a manatee

Cocky as Long John Silver bluffing,
Jawing to Kathy, pale from miscarriage, and to me
Of Allen's twins,

How a son had strangled. Then
Laughing and coughing you
Set course for Quincy's guest suite bathroom,

Your chin crooking as if to hold a violin.
Uncrowned, unvanquished
Your landed mind held court.

Your loving friends took care always,
Fanny and Grey, Bingo, Elizabeth, Bill
Though you are gone still willing

To lend the hand you never could take.
The river by Dunbarton flows
Seaward, luminous, calm in its wide banks,

Steady into the growing dark
Where the Russian poet your friend
Friend only of your poems now

Ponders the stones and the chance flower,
Backing away to the city, to the perilous
Passions of those you commanded to love.

Christo's Fence

Falling, to the insistence of gravity,
The sun from horizon touches the ivory
Felt of tall-crowned hats,
Sundown through Christo's dreaming
Fence that wimples
Oxblood over
The fawn dunes below of merino
Sheep folds and Marin rock
Of goat-gray seabound light crashing
Softly against the windburned
Face of the rancher
Continuous with this place: he

Looks forth on pool, field, flock, mute
Luminous seam. Handy,
Ready, I want to look at, to ask him
What leaves he turns
In the vellum binding of choices made.
"I want to do this thing," wind buffeting
With calm firmness over
Him surviving the time he created,
Time he lives across, "I
Want to do the best thing." What
Else to know; men
In the corridors of their haste
Smiling with a wrinkle
At corners of a mouth that seems
For a moment to crumble a little,
Bits of crimson over the chin and bola
Tie like wine spilled; wanting to go

Back, back to the shagreen
Pasture where the posts stood
More in the pull
Of the wire than tall on a punky foot?

Continuous with the time
He hovers, the sheep lapels
Of coat smoulder
In the twilight wind, difficult man
Watching light dapple
The swooping skirts. The past
Passes like a helicopter of the state,
Free of feeling, checking
Him out, between the wind
And trammeled grass beneath our boots.

Rural Affairs

for Stanley Hyman

Between the groves of maples
Where locusts are zithering and the barn downhill
Where the pigeons croon and lull themselves
From their contented throats, a column
Of asparagus beetles swarms,
The swirl distinct in air above the tendrils
Of asparagus galaxy gone to seed.

Their songs are joined
By the groan of vans climbing the hill
And the farmer, turning his mower home.
They close one movement, task, day.
Now you are gone, and in this world
We'll have no more of your invitations,
No drinks on your veranda.

The horizon shows our battle monument's
Shaft in haze, like a translucent rocket,
Waiting. No, do not call it an erection
Of granite—or, just now, apparently of glass—
That is too brittle to suggest
Life, life wavering
A little in the summer heat;

In my opinion—you would have said—
Comparison of monuments to sexual
Rousings is not
Helpful. Our distant obelisk is no
Use, a pillar built to men too long ago

Fallen in battle; like an ancient drachma,
No longer legal tender.

The throttled air blends with our Russian olive,
Silver, wistful, draped with dusty creeper.
Through the heat, the city spread down valley is a blur
Where children, too wired after supper there
To notice any heat except their own
Will yell and gather
Running or biking in the blistering air.

The White Oak of Eagle Bridge

Below the house it reached its black arms across the sky.
Those arms spread—you might think if you stood under them—
horizon to horizon; at least from the peak of my roof
to the milk shed across the road. There I stood and watched
from its long veranda of shade my field over the road
being mown and raked. One year I went down to lend a hand,
the summer Joseph's rake broke down, the sheaves gathering
sunlight as they rose to the gray, longsleeved arms
of Joseph Judd, his collarless cotton shirt buttoned,
then to the arms of his wife blue-jeaned against hay dust
but working along with him, Mr. and Mrs. Joseph
Judd the season through like cheerless speechless workers
of Breughel, row by row cutting, loading their wagon,
carrying eight acres of hay in their old arms.

Another year, for taxes, they sold Treddle their mare
for whom they worked the field. No stopping for coffee now,
courtly half hour in the kitchen when the Judds,
brushed clean, had done receiving the hay: it had been barter,
I gave good hay for their good work. They stayed at home,
a cape of tarpapered clapboard down by the Hoosac. I watched
the field go white with daisies, yellow with buttercups;
lavender off to the left, chicory mixing with purple
clover; mallow, splotches of vetch; and soon the popple
saplings, blinking with light: no good for haying now,
or not until someone ploughed, if someone wanted to.

One August when the wind leaned on the oak and nudged
the crown an inch or two off plumb, more than was well
with gravity, it leaned and, creaking, leaned more yet

as if peering over an edge, and fell. I walked, I walked
in tears, as if a friend had died. I saw that hollow,
and ants that swarmed the sawdust the town crew left behind
when they cleared the road for traffic. So much firewood,
pitiful sight! Presence of rotting light stormed down
and occupied the whole place: where the burled limbs
had always made a lichened, shaggy pagoda of tree;
brackets of lesser branches, bunches of scalloped leaves
that chittered in winter together. An alien light blinded
the thin acidulous grass on the slope, burned out the veins
five kinds of mushrooms bulged from after a summer shower.

I waited for something to happen, as if one night the tree
wearing the whole garment of its former harmony
would return with just the same shock and simplicity
of its fall, the old dark of its arms webbing the moonlight
that fell on the slope like snow, like the spongy sepulchral
luminescence of wood rotting.

                    Another year went by,
the persistence of the oak still made its absence felt
as strongly as when it stood there and made its presence known
on the slope, the benediction of its choosing *here*
to have stayed on, regardless of weathers, not building a name.
As strongly as the absence of Joseph and Mrs. Judd
who, silently as they worked hayload after hayload,
had left their river place; bedroom and stable, shed
and parlor, scarved in tar shingle and climbing rose,
windows boarded, a mullein tall in the dooryard one day
when I walked down to the Hoosac for the great blue herons.

I took the back way home and met my neighbor, Myron,
still farming at eighty-three and still the town assessor.
We remembered old Joe Judd and Mrs. Judd and wondered
where they had gone, and how they lived without this place
and how—for that matter—they had managed with it.
"Judd was always a blank," said Myron, "on our tax roll."
In front of my place now we paused; Myron brought up
that oak. "It had a sickle left hanging in it. Slowly
swallowed, probably, by the growing. Probably
still there. Unless the chainsaw came across it and sent it
flying." And old man Judd, I asked him, what of Judd?
"Well, there's a couple! Don't you worry, they'll do well.
Now your white oak," said Myron, who'd lived the next farm up
now eighty years, "you know, your white oak stood beside
another one, exactly like it, girth and crown.
'Twin Oaks' they called your place."

                        He'd always thought of them
as twins, he said, but saw no point in telling me
a thing from his own childhood when there was only the one
I knew about. I found no trace of the ancient stump;
Myron had forgotten just where that mirror twin,
invisible perfect tree, had stood, matching what's now
a jagged center where the dark shaft rose beside
the field filling with goldenrod to a man's height;
popple getting a start; asters; nobody's field.

II

Expecting Fathers

"It's not the way it was supposed to be,"
The laboring mother muttered when the neuter
Light plumed on paper toweling, fluorescent medley
Of edges in the hall half laundry and half lab.

The play-offs make more sense. Dads eddy, cowed,
In the TV lounge. They want something they can handle.
No padded diapers, their boys wear shoulder pads.
Then what is this, a cameo appearance by a primate?

I put him down too fast on the bunting in the cradle
Near the stove he'll sleep beside. His arms startle,
Reach up, catching at air; the fingers clench,
The Moro reflex, reaching for a branch.

I hear the tiny yodel, a far blood-curdling yell
As if he called out to me, shouted in fear
A half a field, not half a yard, away.
I sit back, drawing great blanks on the years to come.

From Away

Later, at evening, on Route 90
The lavender coma of Iowa
Twilight, sluggish cornfields float
On snow to the inky flats of the creeping
Dinosaur valleys behind us.
Weary of mileage, the child

Is dozing through the news: "God
Gives burdens," the President
Is drawling, "but He
Gives shoulders, too."
I am driving westward
And look to her, the skinny

Scapula of my child's body, feeling
A terror in this: and I look back
At the blipped tornado of a speeding bus;
And soon the boy on the roadside, thumbing; his hopeful
Stance, the looking-good, the peerings
Into the wind at everyone oncoming.

I mind the wheel
While this thriving body near me breathes in a dream.
I know how the President is drowsing, half
Dead to the world, his cares grown small
As a distant smudge of storm on the horizon.
We are all sleeping,

Like the child who startles
Only at sudden swerves or thunder-flap
Of a trailer passing near. Because
Of us, I am glad to the brink of fear
And death is only
Decibels, like abandonment.

The Sunday Outboard

To the right from the head of the water now
The grinding burble of an outboard through
The spruce crowding the shore; and now the boat
Emerged, nibbling into view, brimming with people,
A dark bouquet of heads against the light-
Slabbed surface; working left toward town
And the disused steamboat channel—no doubt fetching
The Sunday papers. It passed as if in haste.
Then nothing for minutes of blank silence, one
Pigeon hawk sailing across the upper lefthand
Corner of the sky. Soon the wake of the outboard
In parallel swells dashed the shore, broadside
At his feet, splashing in strokes scumbled with light.

The boat just gone, whose absence now was touching
Him at the edges of the medium
Through which it drove, would make him think of them
—He, she, all of them—placid, day by day
Unmoving as a pond in autumn hills
Until one morning they see how something's passed
Through them; commotion hatching at the edges.

Take the daughter, one day no longer hanging
On his neck in wonder. She has taken note
Of *the sexy parts*, goes off under the eaves
By herself as if forever, without a doubt
Offended seeing how things were at home:
The roof of care they had to shield her with,
Only a token shelter from the brawn
Of avenues, or talk heard on a street.

How long he sat there with lake for company
Escaped him, till from the silting steamboat channel
The far whine of the boat returning reached him.
The papers, he thinks, and comics for the kids.
Into the light-spill on the glassen calm
The outboard cuts a fine loud swath: as if
In haste heading up lake now, droning into
The palisade of spruces, out of sight.

The News and the Weather

Equal to each unknown, our TV oracle
Foretells a heat wave in Washington; a storm
For New Hampshire. Yesterday, he cast this spell:
The earliest frost in years for the Green Mountains,
Berkshires, Taconics; an August ice age. I culled
The ready fruits and spread bedsheets, one
For tomatoes, one for the grapevine by the wall.
Anchored edges with stones; in a rising wind,
Hosed down the tents. My son, how he bellowed, leapt
With the gusts, hurtled with glee!
                                        This morning, sun
Is on the begonias; wet light beads the apples,
Tomatoes and peppers beam. It's summer still.
The phone rings softly, like the steeple bell
Down valley. You have no news, you're only asking
The date of your grandson's birthday. I tell you, mother,
For talk, the weather; how no frost came last night.

Reading of the Black Death and Watching the African Famines on TV

*Y. Pestis, carrier of Plague, did not infect
horses. Plague gave unafflicted towns the
opportunity to attack the afflicted.*

Terrain I had my eye on,
That rural Pistoia Florence eyed,
Had shrunk to ten thousand and horse,
A scanted landscape the ill flea canceled.

That rural Pistoia! Florence eyed
A state of barred towers, naked men,
A scanted landscape the ill flea canceled
Of numb mouths swallowing helplessly,

A state of barred towers. Naked men
Dwindled to char, the hacking gargle
Of numb mouths swallowing helplessly,
Innocent monuments to a power they could not see.

Dwindled to char, the hacking gargle,
Rats clotted the streets, bloated like wineskins,
Innocent monuments to a power they could not see.
People changed things, the old cult of new stars;

Rats clotted the streets, bloated like wineskins;
Nature, the Almighty's vicar, squealed with laughter.
People changed things, the old cult of new stars,
Scarcely if ever for the better.

Nature, the Almighty's vicar, squealed with laughter;
Swellings in the groin, in the armpits, and no warning.
Scarcely if ever for the better
Change overtook the dynasties in their senility,

Swellings in the groin, in the armpits, and no warning.
The effect of new patrons was visible soon,
Change overtook the dynasties in their senility.
Warm, sympathetic, art had stressed personal bonds;

The effect of new patrons was visible soon,
The cypress no longer shaded a mother washing her child.
Warm, sympathetic, art had stressed personal bonds;
Now all wore the gruesome mask of pain.

The cypress no longer shaded a mother washing her child.
Did Death follow me, a walker charting the streets
Now all wore the gruesome mask of pain?
Not as an airy skeleton, but as a simple figure in black

Did Death follow me, a walker charting the streets?
Did I desire that year too much to possess it?
Not as an airy skeleton, but as a simple figure in black
I stayed on, waiting for an abandoned house.

Did I desire that year too much to possess it?
No mountain ridge, no island stemmed the revel of calamities.
I stayed on, waiting for an abandoned house
Wondering, was the next city safe; city I did not know.

No mountain ridge, no island stemmed the revel of calamities,
Terrain I had my eye on
Wondering, was the next city safe; city I did not know
Had shrunk to ten thousand and horse.

Last Days at York Manor

BEING THERE

That treeless Christmas in their sixth-floor rooms
Of the high-rise luxe retirement Shangri-la
I waited, mostly speechless, and without a gift
Or time for shopping, absently gazing down
At streetlamps and their halos on the asphalt
That light flurries were shading in with white,
Terrain it seemed just now was cornfield where
All summer long I hoed the rows or bagged
The tassels and pollinated sweet-corn ears
For Northrup King; country of old sand roads
And roller coaster sandpits hiding the three-inch
Lake country agates waiting for a rockhound
And his boy; stretches of scree and seedy talus
Effaced for suburbs with one-way boulevards.
The snow laced up the courses of glazed brick
Facade, wrapping the half-excavated park
And a high-tech glass substation of Control
Data. Under an olive sky, the new fields;
White-out for Christmas; for us, and her swathed
In the extended care facility.

SHOPPING

I take a morning drive to look for things,
Eavesdrop at coffee on two who will exchange
The gold chain for a goose-down skiing vest.
In innocent German accent and blond plume

He is ready to hotdog, to buy the whole mall,
At the little table loudly intimate
With his mother, whose admiring reserve
Sheds credit on him. A silver cigarette
Smoulders in her hand raised just between them.
I have come to buy presents for my parents
And cannot find a thing they could possibly want.
I remember her smiling in her chintz chair, looking,
Wondering when the bulldozers would get there
And carve away the hill that blocked her view,
Mountain of glacial till developers
Still promised would become the promised park.

CAROLING

Such weeks, such weeks that might be years;
The upbeat omens keep; lengthen
Like prairies. Good Jeff the waiter shows
A jello belly when he bends
Among the cactuses and wheelchairs,
And the inmates of apartments wait
Held hostage by the cold, the winter
Solstice, and dark that stirs at last;
The week held hostage to the year;
Nativity. The infant Christ
At the ceiling near a cornice, blinded
By spotlights in the showcase lobby,
Hangs bound in shiny swaddling like
A Della Robbia china *bambino*,

Blue and white; hovers above us,
A thousand-and-one nighties the wrong size
Where silvered baubles bedeck blue perms,
Trimmings to pack again in shoeboxes
On wardrobe shelves come New Year's Day.

PATIENCE

He had come in from the parking lot and heard
    The counting, the soft voice
Counting. If when he heard he went to her,
    His dazzled retina turning

Negative her bath—the towel, the tile
    And her, huddling there
Bald as a baby on the floor, one wild
    Finger prodding her waste—

Helping her back to rest would take no skill
    As if that act of pity
He moved through were a take from an old film
    And he was quieted

To sense a presence with more pain than theirs
    Had held and dealt those tears.

DECOY

With son and father talking, it's no trouble
Killing time. The duck with glass eyes stares,
Shellacked, between them on the carpet; gift
Of old Ted Freeman, who years ago skinned off
The painted feathers (where now we see a great
Lead slug wedged in for ballast) and christened it
A doorstop. Once more he praises me for what
I hardly possess and—out of modesty
Or guilt; or truth—stoutly deny. So why
Are we talking about poetic meter and
Poetic form? Our lives are late for *belles lettres*.
We've known each other forty years and more.
Was it so hard so long to show some life?
But he will inquire again about rhyme scheme,
What rhyme is, honestly now, beyond the sound.
I will respond, rhyme is as when his thought
Resembles a thought his father had, just as
Though my face is mine, all see my father in it.
I might tell him a rhyme is when a man
Becomes a father, but then he'd say something
About a scheme and have me falling silent
And watching my daughter, now playing with the duck.
The mallard's a doorstop, but truly it had been
A decoy, "perhaps a Joe Lincoln," people said,

And had it not been stripped today worth thousands;
Not one of the replicas machines engender.
He quotes me Shakespeare and Sam Pepys; his art
Of conversation highballs past midnight through
The room, the green-eyed mallard on the pond
Of carpet by his grandchild, exhausted girl,
In sleep touching her imagined bird.

THE PARK

Another day, I look from the sixth-floor window
At the sumac and barberry clumps that crown the hill
Directly opposite. Then I step out
On the little triangular balcony crowded
With pots of geranium stalks and stare across
At a family of pheasants lounging in snowy
Bowers, behind which rises the turret of
The construction company's sand mill, its great scoops
Trundling earth six storeys up to sift
Into great cones below that wait for dump trucks.
The pheasants are motionless and look as if
They're looking my way. I think that battlement
Looks lower this winter than last year, but it
May be this snow, or just imagination;
Or the sense of time thinning everything down,
Like the winded flanks of the half buried Sphinx.

Headland

The snow fell at length
Like a gift
To cover
His journey; the worn

Hermit post; his
Path in time.
More to fear than this
Brief time to break

Camp was that
Last encounter shaking
Hands by the shaded
Lamp; briefly your

Boy making his way
To you and you
Man torn then
Toward friend

Pulling still
With more to fear than
This knowing about
Being over, father.

◆

Dropped in
This field
By love,
Which did

Not cease
But passed
Onward
Like the winter

Falling back now
Down to
The developed
Horizon

Smoke
Beckoning, you
Rise at hand
Pinching my sleeve

With nailed
Fingers numb
And move
Around my

Attention now
Like the sparrow
Hawk, high
Out the window,

Slowly
Circling the forenoon
Of small shadows;
High noon

That illustrates
The white
Hoard of his home, his
High headland.

Station 41

It is the last stage of day. The bending sky
Streams west; the final peels of peachblow cloud
Drift back. Snowfields below like tarnished brass
Give up a brightness as blues shade them. I
Alone and westward wend behind a crowd
Of men unwinding, each flying business class
With complimentary glass of wine or malt or gin;
After quotidian
Foray, making joyful the noise of return.
I will not see them, grinding at the quern
Of going to the old home, but hear their voices
Like gulls above the stern
Of my ship as it makes for port and the few choices.

Like sparklers on Twelfth Night thrown to the snowy dark
The Swede towns flicker bravely and go out
Five miles below on the sable parcels of night.
The Pratt & Whitney afterburners spout
Fire, then purr: descending through an arc
The aircraft touches down. End of flight.
Hardly a proselyte of heaven or anything
Like it, I stand in a ring
Of passengers waiting for baggage, crowding like swine
In a pen: I'm shaken to see, when bags of mine
Crash down the chute, how time the foreman picks
And chooses from the line
Of travelers in Minnesota at the Styx.

Who the man is, and how lonely lying here
Hobbled and cribbed in the elevator bed,
I can't imagine. Nobody. Anyone,
Whose silver hair unfolds from the slackening head
On pillow; no senator or financier
But boy fallen among Cadillacs; no fun
To find himself the one responsible, the boss,
At last not at a loss
For words. "Tea kettle ... burglar ... Spanish War ..."
He slushes now in a voice half sigh half snore;
Cries then, "kill the rest"; defiance flashes
In his eyes as never before;
And kicks a nurse before his anger crashes.

With my brother and sister I stood
On the dock admiring the string of fish he held
Up for the camera
And us. He spoke that way
Or danced the messages
In tap shoes on the kitchen floor
Or said the Philadelphia Grapevine on his skates;
Preached elegance behind the wheel
As when he steered between the car he passed
And the moving-van oncoming.
He'd take his skates, the tap shoes
And the Shakespeare he had thumbed for years
And as he climbed the stairs
Flick off the lights, whatever

It was we were doing down there canceled.
Together we across the lake
Watched while he came heading in
Over the waters of Minnetonka,
Like Teddy Roosevelt on horseback
Careening down San Juan Hill;
Our father moving tall across the waves.
He stood in the rowboat, performing the forbidden;
His Johnson Seahorse outboard blustering on,
Whining when the hull slammed down
On the wakes of other fishermen who traipsed
Across this bay and that
Like little lords amain the sea
Making their names by conquering
The sunfish and the bass
As if freshwater fish were Spanish galleons;
Fathers in panamas on Sunday cruises,
Whole afternoons spent out of earshot, far
From the families on level lawns above the sand.
Through the lapis welter of the day
He came ashore,
The outboard idling to the dock;
Fixing us with an admiring eye,
His smile bursting us ajar, as he
Without a word held up his catch.

He is talking again now, about elephants.
How they sway with dignity and make their way

On cushioned soles, their little sleepy eyes
Alert. The creased, terrain-like skin. The gray
Which doesn't show the dirt, a circumstance
Pleasing to God, no doubt. And in their sighs
The smell of hay. That wise strength and magnificence
Swayed by obedience
To the man wielding a goad. A sneak attack
Of dozing takes him: five minutes, and he's back.
Out the window, he sees an old man with a girl.
They're doing the Zodiac,
He says. I watch the snowfall gust and swirl.

We did not turn (this was the dream) to drive
Around the block and back to our front door
But veered into a park, bucking the curb
Into the dark, where soldiers of the Great War
Stole past us, benighted silhouettes alive
With strobelike backflares, wary not to disturb
A wire or the superb composure of a mine,
The quiet kindled by the whine
Of an occasional artillery shell above.
You drove smoothly as ever, cognizant of
Each chuckhole; tightlipped, intent, cruising along
Without speech for love
Or me, into that stealthy, helmeted throng.

What time leaves behind is the high-tech of things.
Fat tubes like tentacles coil up from bruising

Needles in forearms to floats bobbing above
Two red-eyed volumetric pumps infusing
Lidocaine hydrochloride (which sweetly brings
Peace to the heart agitating for love)
And other potions of heal-all technologies
Which counter the disease
Of age, raise flesh from its stupor on the floor,
Proffer the derelict a coat, and pour
The life-supports—sucrose, potassium,
Heparin sodium chlor-
ide—into him, hot coffee for the homeless bum.

From the skewed mouth with a kind of howl
He mumbles, "damn you you are being cruel."
I wonder if he smells the mustard stench
Lapping everywhere. We're back at school,
Learning to hold still with Atenolol.
He claws at his monitor and tries to clench
It in his fingers, wrench it loose. The box that warns
If heart should fail adorns
His chest like an Olympic medal. In a blur
I see his sex lying there, too faint to stir,
Gray in a condom, cuffed with a little strap
Attached to a catheter;
Like a dead mouse in gray grass, head in a trap.

In teal shadows where breezes scarcely shook
The oak leaves, against the furrowed gray

Bark seamed with a moss inlay,
I saw him leaning with his book
Far from the machines
Of endless learning;
Delivered from routines.
He was returning
When he put down *The Merchant* and surveyed
The sultry field with daisies simmering
In the blue, replenishing
Midday. The day grew quiet by a hundred stages,
Scored with the braid
Of a blackbird's call
From cattails by the brook.
The singing there was small,
And the abandoned book
On its back lay open wide,
The breeze leafing slowly through the pages.

How I came slowly to his going then!
I heard the nurse long-distance telling me
The mottling and the cyanosis had begun.
I would not comprehend the urgency,
He was so strong, headstrong; strongest of men,
He'd stay among his three at least till one
At bedside, daughter or son,
Hugged him to speech, to bless
From his high wilderness
His child; but toiled then, now with joke, now rage.
At last it was mine to be next: to disengage

And sing, as the tenor, called to his loveliest
Work, brightens the stage
Alone and sings, by the dark hall possessed.

III

Day Care for Lover

He sits in the Coffee Shop *Peekaboo*
In the beat of traffic that encroaches
Through nylon curtains. Little wiser
For the hour spent tracking the roaches glossing
The *faux marbre* terrain of veined
Congoleum, he falters, brained
By Tokyo; but will wait till he spies her,
Pinned by the arrow of time. And she
(Like an apparition then) approaches
Among the tables. She holds his hand
Palm up; her finger traces his *kanji*
For today: the seven strokes of the new
Meaning, the new character, crossing
The life and fate lines of his pale hand.

After a City Shower

The traffic brays, but the stalled horses
Calmly stare, exhaust in their nostrils,
As if they were hearing the wind's bel canto
In tall grass. Out of the horns of plenty
Banter drifts near *A La Vieille*

Russie: "move out," she tells him, "so don't
Go back." Her voice turns liquid, "allow me
To send you some." The silver parcels
And the practiced tintinnabula of hungers
Surround me; as much as wisdom I desire

The white rush of this intersection;
To take the meaning, once, of the corner
Of fashion. Tune to the man in gray flannel.
"Few people knew the true gentility
Of the czar and the czarevitch. But that

Was when." In the square the Beaux Arts fountain
Tumbles its effervescent helix
Of waters heaping, fogging the air
With scoops of mist that rise and vanish
In the brandy shadow of the Plaza's frieze.

On the blacktop where rainbows from oildrip mix
In puddles the rain left, people wait
For the light, then make their crossings. The Black,
Laboring, kindled, leans into his own
Saxophone gold by the fountain's pool,

And I hum with him, hum his keening,
Lost so and found among the obsidian
Limos; one high, gridlocking strain
While twilight fords Manhattan, whose
Splayed wires thread each longing gaze.

Dinner for Two

The subtle and the obvious entwined
As they negotiated while they dined
Together. Other patrons, polyglot
Among the tables, faded, babbling prose,
Leaving them diachronic; at home with lines
Recalled across a silence.
                       They had these lines
So old they seemed a home away from home.
Both melodies converged till one song rose
Like Venus, single from vociferous foam.

He feels he is running in place, pounding one spot,
His meaning being given, slowly, to love.
He is sweating. Distances always were pantomimes
Of credibility; when he moved toward them
They receded: or, as now, they fade and seem
To be what, earlier, was not. Sometimes
The mountain, on near inspection, becomes a glove;
The credible mountebank, a visored cloud;
The cloud, cloud-capped, becomes another cloud.
And she, first one foot then the other, slowed
In her place. Maybe she never ran for it, or jigged
Her jig. Familiar distances would fade
Into the latest view. The difference it made!
She began to think her whole part had been rigged.

Poor lovers, bargaining from privileged heads!
Their narrative typology was dead,
Roughly. For company, each brought a dream;
And all their variations drowned the theme.

Cabbage Days

Look how in heat waves the folding metal
Chairs go slack in the sun
And their withered arms settle
Waiting like ritual tongs to hold your body.

How their legs puncture the lawn
And the grass lies back, creeps on.
Think how the comfrey and mint
Will grow and cleave

Till it's time to bolt.
Look how the cabbages swelled
And now it is time to loosen carefully,
To give the feeder roots a severing jolt

With a twist of each head on its stalk
Detaining green
Increase in holding patterns
Until it is time to take them in.

Think how you, supple
On long afternoons, have lain in the sun
Or stood up
Glad not to be of use, not to be held.

Picnic with Morgan

for Roger Rath

Sitting high there in the spray,
Folding our cellophane, we're almost
Out of earshot. We keep

Quiet, let the falls do
The talking, voluble palaver
Off there we keep an eye on,

Tympanic hubbub that keeps us sheepish
Around all this white water, this
Glacial milkshake, shy

As if the torrent's ear, like
A mike boom, hovered barely
Out of sight in the hornbeam that clings

To the rock above. The ice chest
Is full, sandwiches, wine, your sandwich
Bag of weed. We move closer,

We have the whole day and sprawl
On any moss ledge, broadloomed outcrop.
I hear him clear his throat

As if to call attention from the cliff
Of soothing babble, but Morgan says
Nothing. Pours wine in a tin cup;

Turns again to the waters.
A lot of room here for the water
Confetti that sticks to the rockery,

A scaled-down diorama of black shale
Glassy with droplets that creep along
Minute ridges, deltas of lichen. A drop

Runs giddy, snaking its way; gathers; then
Descends to a toothpick limb
Of Wall Rue, or the lime

Stuffed cushion of a mullein leaf.
I call to him, "what do you say?"
He watches as if he listened

For what the water might be telling.
I thought he probably was remembering
Waves of his childhood, drum-rolling

The length of beaches of New South Wales.
Morgan had something, always, to say.
But that noon his lips were sealed.

He waved at me like a passing surfer
Risking a moment of balance,
Making me wish I had not spoken.

Again, the gentle din between us
Down that adhesive mist. A reckless
Parcel of spray scooped by the wind

From the plunging water crossed him,
A modest drop hung at his eyebrow.
On rocks as aquiline as those

One of us could have shed
A tear and the other never know;
Or tell, among those speaking stones,

If the tear was of sadness or laughter.
"Sincerity," he said just then.
I hear it still, the word called out as if

He had hallooed for a hermit of that name
Whose hut the cliff beside that fall
Sheltered. He turned to me

And startled as if he thought he'd been alone.
He smiled now, then he turned
To pour the wine. We raised our cups

And drank each other's eyes. He lay back
And spoke once more of 1929,
Garcia Lorca

Living in Eden Mills
Not half an hour from where we sat,
How a poet, a stranger in America,

"In a state of desperation very hard"
Walked the straw terror of these hills
Down a forgetting August, dry

And drained as a blossom rinsed
In the murderous sun of Granada.
We drowsed a sleepy hour then

Or half an hour, we did not count.
I watched him waken shivering,
Sit up and press his eyes; he says,

"I thought this was going to be summer.
The story of my life.
Packing a foam cooler of ice

To the head of freezing Mansfield Glen,
Cold as a penguin's foot all year."
Laughter, restrained on hands and knees,

Peering down into lucid rock a foot away
Past lichen and glint of schist and spar,
We look at stone as if

Through water to a creekbed, crawling back
After a piss to our old places,
Creeping like creatures quickening

In the wet shade of the covering wall
To lower forms of life.
"How still it is right here," I say.

"You think so," he cries. Then edging
To the brink he kneels, peers over, calls,
"Not to worry about a thing,

Everything will turn out right."
And edges back to say, "let's turn our cards in:
Tear up your cards; sail them

Into the water." He's slinging plastic; then
He freezes; like the wave, caught
Like a bone in the throat of its own motion.

From dawn to sundown in this spot
A cold shade reigns that does not pass.
Already shadows deepen. The afternoon

Light is dwindling above. He pours
A cup of the red for each of us
And sidles near. He speaks

Below the torrent in a whisper.
"I did not say truth here,
But desire; not

Plain dealing but
My own need." He cuffs me,
He distances himself,

Composes himself
Again sitting in silence. A surf
Of spray, stuck there

Like tinsel of the sun,
Froth on the petal of the flesh.
His poem about Lorca,

The graveyard in Eden, Vermont.
High on the southeast corner
I would be placed, under one weather.

Quick from the other side of the world,
Threading the rifled barrel of a wave
He came, tilting the board, long ago.

What might a surfer do in mountains,
Arms held wide, the nut brown knees
Flexed at the right bend, all the body

As if to embrace the whole sunlight?
We said nothing, I think we saw
How the waterfall felt,

The difficulty a river has
Getting along in alien country
Preferring not to have to act up,

Put on this astonishing show
Just to get down
And be a stream again.

IV

Landscape with the Body of Judas

The sunflowers bowed their heads. Insects. A new moon
And a house with eyes. The leaves were down, the wind
Had come by the house, where late apples bobbed
On the branches. An aged crone in an aged coat

Would pace each day down Hill Street, staring at me
As if I were November. *On your way*, she cried once,
As though I had tried her daughter. Dürer might have
Drawn her, or these arthritic exquisite twigs

The wind palsies, the gray light tangled in gray
Gnarling of branches drooping, hanging slack
Where the feverish apples glow and thirst. A frayed
Clothesline hangs down, where a child has tied a Raggedy

Andy, waterlogged now, livid; the body
Heavy, a bloated purse. I remember the woman's hand
Brandished a staff of light that shed age-spots
On her skin. Her coat was quilted with righteousness.

The Man of Mogador

On the glassy gravel and the grassy
Shoulder of Turnpike Road I sauntered
One afternoon without a cloud
And as I walked I listened. Just
When I heard the alders rustle

As if something I could not see
Was standing there or coming through
An old man in an old car came speeding,
White hair flying, toward me, driving
West into a sun nine feet wide

And from the gaping mouth I saw
The man was laughing, or crying out.
At the rise where I am standing, when
He meets the exact sacrificial
Reflex of a Northern Grouse

Flapping in front of the car, his wheel
Swerves; when the steel glares he brakes
—the sun flare mounts right up
The hood—impales him then
Blinds him to the file of fledglings

She is leading his glance from.
The rasping gravel whirrs and now,
One moment, stillness; stillness.
Such stop-frame stillness I had not beheld
Since I, drawn to the spectacle,

Pulled over once near Mogador
To watch: a lone man on a bare hill
Stand motionless, slow minute
By slow minute, only the black
Djellabah the wind touched, lapping, lapping.

The fledglings toddled from the blacktop
To the shoulder, from gravel down to mustard,
Alder, shadow; after the mother
To cover of shade, scrawling a slow
Maneuver of survival. The driver

Gunned his engine and sang out something
I could not get; and I often wonder
What on earth he was speeding after
As he went, his tires spitting sand
With the weight of his voice and laughter.

Allegheny Front

Out of the dark, from a field over the valley, a cow calls.
In the quiet, the hoarse lowing crumbles from her throat
And fades. Silence again; each barn and star holds still.
Perhaps that voice the Allegheny hills echoed
Told of some pasture matter, or did it, late on the Sabbath
As the midnight drew near, declare a purge from the simple
Darkness of the traditions of men, the passing away
Of laws that had come to pass? I sensed the 1880

Town devout, how near each felt: the obedience
In holding hands; each channel free of interference
From tape, free of the tube unborn, not yet branding
Cerebral hemispheres with circuits indelible
As rust. In the glass negatives from the house on Main
That my friend printed, half the town—and two cows—pose,
The set jaws sweet. Those bumptious Chaucerian Baptists loved
Their fun but hadn't much, each gent his own Chanticleer.

But justification burgeons like sheaves bound in the rich
September of their fields, enough to make homes rosy
Through bellowing winters from Canada. The girls have scrubbed
And changed, entered; sat, stifling giggles, hands palm down
On taffeta skirts as if wiping, or spreading patterns;
The shopowner's coat, an upholstered tent, hangs off his body.
Mothers in pleats and ruchings of jet and blue cohere
In the chevrons of their blood. With no rouge or powder, faces

Shimmer as if the humidest day of summer chose them
To sit still or stand without moving, this task of recording
Saved for a day one stood there and watched the corn grow.

Perhaps their faces are glowing with other fire, celestial
Preenings, a sweat of salvation. The Spirit quickens, it whispers
In the pew, the surrey; it beats in the milkhouse pungent with curds
And sawdust in darkness; nasturtiums peek in at the door.
A visage looks on when they try on shoes and bend to peer

In patent leathers mirrored in polished blindnailed wood.
I was watching Emmanuel's land, where springs embroidered with vetch
Assemble, brim to trickle and stream to the still river
Where water, in shade of oak or storefront, flows or pools
By Main Street; falls two feet, crosses under a bridge
And courses on down-valley; mutters in white by mossy
Boulders, lapping the winding hillsides ruddy with clover,
Zoned with sheep. The thick-rumped fathers of Kankadea

Allowed the righteous to settle, swank as well as lame.
They would lay much aside at home; they became their ledgers,
Recorded each occasion, every possession; they
Had eggs on the spit, they were hunky dory; muscular
Never to hear what other men had done or were doing
In other places of the earth. The valley they chose
Smiled from limestone, cleaved to fossils of bivalve and snail;
And the paper of trellised flowers behind the nonagenarian

Is proved to be scored and peeling by the light raking
From the window with curtains parted at the left of the picture.
The family at the farm has spread a tablecloth of damask
On the lawn before they pose on it. Churches are plain
With little spires of tin, but the churches are many
And none abandoned. "Children," the minister cries, "can tell

Cheese from chalk, they know by God's grace how every kite
Has two requirements for flight: the wind that holds it high

And string to be rudder and guide its way; to be anchor
And hold it down. What is that string? Who holds that string?
Who can tell us today?" The pint-sized pinafored girl
Has been catechized, she flounces up the aisle beaming.
"The string is the Ten Commandments. Our Lord holds the string."
Her eyes rake the faithful, quaffing their approval.
The church, a barn with Greek trim nailed to the front, hulks,
A canal barge beached at an intersection of county roads

To which through waves of heat some forty or fifty souls
Carefully file, flushed and beleaguered in Sunday attire.
I climb the steps and enter a lobby with shelves of tracts
And a guest book, its thick wings spread. A cadre of ladies gives
An alarm of smiles; fluttering glances grapple among them
To find a stranger. In the heat of the Sabbath each lady
Conveys the militant, rosy assurance of an immortal.
Syrup of electric organ pours forth the *Old Hundredth*,

The minister-for-the-day stumbles among the verses
Of a psalm. One monitoring elder smacks his thigh,
He has taken color photos from his wallet for the Sabbath,
They are shut in the glove box of his Dodge locked in the sun.
The elders fidget, smooth their sky-blue suits and whisper
During a hymn, check out the scattered congregation
As if they are taking note of particular absences,
The stain of green and ocher lights on the pew that curves

Around no one; they pass the brass collection plates
That ring if given anything but folding money.
Over the bare, spackled walls the color of decrepit
Silk some flies randomly pause to lick, the sermon
Echoes as if down a tunnel; in a foreign tongue.
I cannot make out the sense. "One witness shall rise up . . ."
Finding freshwater words for the mouths of brute nature
As flanges hum in the great calefaction of all things

When the wise sunflower of dawn opens over the black
Collar of Allegheny horizon distantly pinned
With silos and crossroads; cumuli gaining shape with light,
Rose brothers of mountainsides. The highway sings,
A prism, the waxed gut of morning up from dreams
Out of the cushioned pews of cloud in rivering olive
Light. Carnelian hills! It is the Lord's Supper
The rough hand draws the dirty cloth from, brassy host

In salvers for his shaking hand. On the Southern tier
Out of the oak and maple woodland, out of the horn
Of modesty, skull and antler, sliced bellies of deer
Flame on the blacktop shoulders in the eyes of crows
On duty, picketing, holding their beaks wide, crowing, flapping
Their great black capes when I drive past. Believe the word
You do not hear. For the pause, the stutter of Sabbath,
Is awkward only, the silences are lively. The gift

Is blind. I kneel down, I begin to pray, I hear
My own authority, cool voice which says that beauty

Bears the numen, spirit rider. I am numb,
I am deaf. Mine are not laws, but feelings that earn
No bread in the milky valley, the pastel poverties
With their electric crosses and rayon memories
Saying grace from vestal mouths. At home, I wash and watch
The water braid to the marble basin, circle and pool.

Steel drums of heat sound overhead, thunders gather
Toward the cells of the monkish towns in mist-shrouded bottoms.
Town fathers plumb their doubts about wind instruments
But allow some laconic brass with fireworks on the Fourth.
It's still illegal on Saturday to stroll on Main,
Yet on Monday I'll find the living-color cards of men
And women coupling, laid back on subway turnstiles, behind
The sumptuous note cards with views of grazing thoroughbreds.

Keen as the semi's scrawl in the ears, swallows score
My sight, looping at evening toward chimneys of Kankadea,
To roofs swaybacked with terra cotta, imbricate tiles
Quoting an ancient world, a Mediterranean South;
Someone is playing a guitar, the melody floats from a Greek
Revival farmhouse. The night is a country church without
An ornament. A cow is lowing in the distance,
And telling the hour a bell in the white steeple answers.

Hesitation at Vermont
Veterans Home

When May had come for keeps the veterans
Who walk out each morning
From the long wings
Took down the guard chain braced in the drive
All the low winter, and I took
My boy to visit
The deer park at Veterans Home.
                              A wizened man there
Wearing a baseball hat
Liked the idea
Of watching a child come up close to the young
Buck whose velveted rack
Looked tender enough,
About to swell, almost tumescent. The deer
Flinched but licked the hand
Of my four-year-old,
Who let him have his way, enthralled by wildness.
The teeth are so small, just like
A person's, he said.
The deer licked him—wet to the elbow. What's
His name? the boy asked then.
Don't have a name,
The old man barked.
                              My boy cannot stop looking
As he comes closer to this
Beyond. He cries then:
Eyeball to eyeball with the steadfast animal.
That deer is nothing but
A pussycat,
The man in the hat declares, a pussycat.

The season is in earnest,
The gate in the fence
Is open now, where deer graze, going through
Their old motions of foraging,
Ceaseless browsing
Though the vets provide their fodder now. The deer
Have nothing to do, nothing
To fear, but now
And then a bawling baby, or an apprehensive
Street-smart kid from Brooklyn,
Or a small boy
Who cries to see what he is watching. The deer
Is patient, or tame, and gives
Great sloppy kisses.

Man in the Open Air

From the hollow, the wind soughing, down there
The mower's engine droned, veneering the slope
With a cloudburst of hay dust
Like a toy twister gaining on the orchard
Where he walked. At length

He stood where the accomplished animals had been
On the cut velvet their green hooves made
Padding long grass to grassy mold,
The neglected garden overthrown
By thistle, daisy, goldenrod. He heard

A cricket tick and watched it press its arms
Against September.
The season turned
In the rainless desert of itself,
Heroic summer canceled like a passion.

Now for the blank of cold, he thought;
Now throw the latch bolt, go and listen
For the chariot in the trees,
The groan of wheels
By the river when the stripped willows whimper

In the wind stroking above. There
In the eyes of limb stubs on the tree trunks
The wheels spin. In the far field
The mower rumbles its cage of blades
Naming the stubble, the cloud of dust.

♦

A ghost settles there, like the ram's
Skull in the grass. Wild carrot
Unfurls through sockets,

Apotropaic stare unblinking, white
And white the chambered horn,
Spiral at last deciduous,

Flowing with bindweed; blown
To the powdery core. Look
Where the skull peers, the altered horn.

◆

After the thunderstorm that night
Everywhere lay the forked, gray falls;
Soggy shuckings, lovely in fracture, strewn
Looking up from the sod as if stunned
Like runners clipped in mid career.

To Bingham Hill's unposted corners
The stripping westerlies reveal
Ebony wristbones of the apple,
The schist ribcage of an elm,
Creases of unmaking in a face.

Off There

Her problem was her problem: nun of nothing,
Standing beside a leaping rivulet that bubbled
Its frothy song in numberless descant,
She listened till she shook with nonchalance,

Her own angel, and dapper with blue-rinsed hair.
She stood as vacant as an uninspired landscape,
Retired and, as it happened, reticent; serene
As a gold leaf, a mind clean as an empty plate

Recalling her welfare check among these birches
And the moss-ribbed streamlet going on and on;
The birch trees athwart as was foretold they'd be;
Tender, as in Russian films or poems of Frost.

The old light drilling at her curled gray hair,
The human heart pausing for whiteness there
Gazed with that easy uselessness of autumn
On her own likeness, unbidden everywhere.

Spider

The redwings have been calling this half hour;
    the sun, falling, will draw away
Their cries. Between the radiator and the sill
    an unhurried spider seems to look,

Wondering where to move. The bodiless head
    —or headless body—holds on to
The legs, a dome of small girders, arching.
    Then gripping the silk line he moves

Out, hand over hand down the grid, over
    and over the spaces set off by lines
Spun from the mouth. He rests before the sting,
    limbs lifting and falling, wrapping, keen

For the firefly mistaken there. The sun,
    beyond, was melting the last braid
Of branches in its eye. It canceled
    each scratch on the window I looked through.

I closed my eyes; there, islands of gold trailed
    across the blackness of closed lids.
The spider tied up his prey; hung there, gainly,
    at rest. The trees are a gray wall

Zoning the world. Downhill, a car speeds through
    the film of the visible. A small
Sublime of violence keeps streaming from him.
    The birds move off, and their song dies.

American Light

Through the expensive century
 Minute miraculars of Kensett
  Sifting green Newport waters
Charged the Third Beach with repose.
 Mooning Blakelock found diadems
  Where Indians encamped in acid groves
Elbowed original stars, the stars

 Fuse, numinous, round each form.
  The faultless clarity of light
A Hill or Church might postulate,
 Luminous untrammeled wild;
  Lane's tremulous Gloucester cove unmoving
Still as Plum Island's flat salt marsh
 Heade regarded and would

 Have folks remember given so
To lumberers, to Bierstadt's filmed
 Scintillant West easy as
  Driven savages to take,
Dissect: yet hardly picturesque
 Where spirit isolate wandered
  Contained, consoled by those

Perspectives improbably receding,
 The only vanishing point beyond
  Beyond. These were correlative
For pioneer profaning limits
 The mental shepherd of his

Dumb hungers, overhanging
Desires extending 'always' out.

Farsighted eye, luminous
    Avenue for one bestial
So helpless urge to bless
    And mutilating to consume
    And evacuating never
To stand, breathe, occupy
    Memorized one space for all

    That too huge hemisphere!
Who settled to take home
    A picture of some picture of it
    Too sensible to that six feet
Amid such waste grace as all
    These fallow these dark starlit
    Valleys would leave to him.

Words for Dr. Richards

"Seduction in a storm
 Of calculating thought
 Must surely be *proper form*
 For bounders. Or it ought.
 (How should I know, here,
 With the heat of rhyme so near?)

"Sentiment's cold, I say.
 Thought makes us energy
 (If you turn it that way)
 And heat. Some won't agree—
 The young man can't, who fears
 The things unknown, the tears.

"New lovers chant and prate;
 Package what's old, what's new
 Outside them; recreate
 What's in it (me) for you,
 In you for me: relations
 That instrument relations.

"Say he's not hard on her,
 Just hard. Make no mistake.
 His tiffs, his lusts were pure;
 No violence is fake.
 An instrument thought played
 She was; a point he made.

"Then level with your lover.
Feel what knowledge you
Find mustering as you hover
Seeing what you're party to
(And the passion growing cold
As intelligence takes hold)."

♦

Old men make testaments
Who know more than they tell.
But few, once done, commence
Their quest again, to dwell
On sense—and referee
Our suspect imagery.

Cold thought could not be true;
Mind's circuitry *not* lame,
Since hot: thought charging through
And through. Don't couple flame
To passion, nor reason freeze.
No identity in these!

The thought that rages right
Renews itself; re-forms
And formulates fresh light.
This man, this heart words warm!
Like the bush burning, thought
That burns does not burn thought.

Thatch

The man with arms who would hold them out
Might not know what a tree he seemed to be
To come for shelter to. Or then one day
He might, as chance decrees; and stop to wonder

Before an oak, inveterate huddler twisting
From storm or reaching sunward on its hill
When it found itself a kind of green veranda
For stragglers, bushed marines combing their hair,

A respite from the hot valley. This
Reticence he'd feel was like the quiet
Of a field when battle has moved onward
Elsewhere, and a strange calm on the long grass

Moves in as if earth shied, wounded, wincing;
And knelt, rooted, for nightfall and the stars.
He thought the reticence like the isolation
Of white dwarves, although a lesser, hardly

Cosmic rigor. He held himself erect.
The grass moved, the crickets in the grass
Stirred then as the grass he trod arched slowly back
Erect as it had been. Night rose; the grass,

The stonecrop, dragon's breath, and yellow asters
Rose up together from advancing shadows
Where the man walked on, imagining the refuge
He would come to, holding his arms wide now

As if to hug the stars, himself the refuge
He plodded toward, finding his body charged
With shade. The dark coursed through him, streamed beyond
Like direct current. Then he thought of those

Who came to him for shelter and how Death
Was his accomplice now, the senior partner;
As once all dwellings had fire only, until
At length the fire and darkness got discarded,

When men stopped watching them; began to live
In the high wattage of what they were doing.
Once, everyone knew thatch, like darkness, like fire,
Presences underfoot or overhead;

Everyone knew them, the rarity of them later
Was only our looking the other way. Only
The reticent man, holding his arms raised wide
Will find it as it was before it went quaint

And fossil, to be killed, like dust. Now he knows it:
Strong as wire, tender almost, a life
Surprised, because it was there all the time
Shy, smiling, asking with its dead lights.

The Heart's Desire of Americans

Squally Election Day, a few drops pebbling
The hood; we wanted a bite to eat but wanted
To vote, to get back to vote; although not voting
Counted, too. We turned in the drive of Concord
Prison, backtracked through drizzle and at the sign
For Walden Pond turned off, on impulse to pay
A visit; parked where a crowd in cars sat talking
In the rain or silently watching it spatter the pond.
Tuesday: they should have been at work. But clearly
They had the day off to vote; and here they were.
Walden, we guessed, had been a glacial kettle
Or the like; since the wooded banks were steep, no way
For the water to get in or out that we could see.
There was a concrete pier with ladders and a beach,
A women's bath house and a men's, and signs that said
"No Swimming." The rain on the wooden rails was beautiful.

❖

Jim said, "I believe everything you say,"
Which made me feel good although I knew of course
There was more than a touch of irony in his voice
And the way he laughed I knew he doubted me
When I told him the last words of Thoreau, as who
Wouldn't. We split a granola bar and decided
To make up proverbs. "He who looks for dustballs
Under the bed is not looking" seemed the most
Likely, here. Goofer feathers, dust puppies, and
Angel fluff we acknowledged as acceptable

Variant wordings for this Concord saw.
We wanted to look, but the rain was not letting up
And still we could not go for coffee without
First changing the old, frayed windshield wipers
For new ones, which he had thoughtfully brought with him,
Some "fits all" kind, not simple to attach at all.

  ◆

Slant capes of rain spilled down and fled, scoring
The dark waters till Walden simmered with light,
While more people arrived in sparkling cars.
Two women in running suits had remembered to bring
A flowered parasol and plain umbrella, which
They put up as they sauntered down the path
Of White Pine needles toward the shore. We decided
Not to waste our time, and be on our way. "Zen mind,
Weekenders' mind," Jim said, and so it seemed.
It was a beautiful time. Even the prison looked
Empty, and the girl at the ice cream counter smiled.
Later, the Deerfield River and its arrangement
Of ice-planed rocks streaming with rain and the late
Twilight gleaming beside Route Two urged us
To stop. And we pulled over. When you've seen
One perfect spot, you want to see them all.

PERMISSIONS ACKNOWLEDGMENTS

Most poems in this work were originally published in the following publications: *The Atlantic, The Bennington Review, Boulevard, Grand Street, Green Mountains Review, Michigan Quarterly Review, NER/BLQ: New England Review and Bread Loaf Quarterly, Quarterly West, Salmagundi, Truck, Virginia Quarterly Review*.

The poem "Spider" was originally published in *The Hudson Review*. The poems "Man in the Open Air" (entitled "Cabbage Days" in this book), "Landscape with the Body of Judas," "Bingham Hill" (entitled "Man in the Open Air" in this book), and "Words for Dr. Richards" were originally published in *Poetry*.

Grateful acknowledgment is made to Monitor Book Co., Inc., for permission to reprint "Man in the Open Air" (entitled "Cabbage Days" in this book) by Stephen Sandy from *Anthology of Magazine Verse & Yearbook of American Poetry—1985*, page 403. Reprinted by permission of Monitor Book Co., Inc., Beverly Hills, California.

A NOTE ABOUT THE AUTHOR

Stephen Sandy was born in Minneapolis and educated at Yale and Harvard. He is the author of three previous collections—*Stresses in the Peaceable Kingdom, Roofs,* and *Riding to Greylock*—and several small-press limited editions. He has been the recipient of numerous grants and awards for his poetry, the Academy of American Poets Prize and an Ingram Merrill Award among them. He has taught at Harvard, the University of Tokyo, and Brown, and is currently on the faculty of Bennington College. He lives in North Bennington with his wife and two children.

A NOTE ON THE TYPE

This book was set in Granjon, a type named in compliment to Robert Granjon, a type cutter and printer active in Antwerp, Lyons, Rome, and Paris from 1523 to 1590. The face was designed by George W. Jones, who based his drawings on a type used by Claude Garamond (c. 1480–1561).

Composed, printed, and bound by Heritage Printers, Inc., Charlotte, North Carolina

Designed by Marysarah Quinn